MW01120447

SCOTTISH TERRIERS

by Martha E. H. Rustad

AMICUS HIGH INTEREST • AMICUS INK

Amicus High Interest and Amicus Ink are imprints of Amicus
P.O. Box 1329, Mankato, MN 56002
www.amicuspublishing.us

Library of Congress Cataloging-in-Publication Data
Names: Rustad, Martha E. H. (Martha Elizabeth Hillman), 1975- author.
Title: Scottish terriers / by Martha E. H. Rustad.
Description: Mankato, Minnesota : Amicus High Interest/Amicus Ink,
   [2018] | Series: Favorite dog breeds | Audience: K to grade 3. | Includes
   bibliographical references and index.
Identifiers: LCCN 2016036531 (print) | LCCN 2016049776 (ebook) | ISBN
   9781681511313 (library binding) | ISBN 9781681521626 (pbk.) | ISBN
   9781681512211 (ebook)
Subjects: LCSH: Scottish terrier--Juvenile literature. | Dog breeds--
   Juvenile literature.
Classification: LCC SF429.S4 R87 2018 (print) | LCC SF429.S4 (ebook) |
   DDC 636.755--dc23
LC record available at https://lccn.loc.gov/2016036531

Photo Credits: eAlisa/Shutterstock cover; Bonzami Emmanuelle/123RF
2, 12-13; JacquilineVanGhent/iStock 5; WikiCommons 6; Robynrg/
Shutterstock 8-9; Olga_i/Shutterstock 10-11; Dina Magnat/iStock 14;
Anna Tkach/Shutterstock 16-17; Harm Kruyshaar/Shutterstock 18-19;
snark/iStock 20-21; Cynoclub/Dreamstime 22

Editor: Wendy Dieker
Designer: Tracy Myers
Photo Researcher: Holly Young

Printed in the United States of America

HC 10 9 8 7 6 5 4 3 2 1
PB 10 9 8 7 6 5 4 3 2 1

TABLE OF CONTENTS

BIG BARK

Bark! Bark! A kid hears a low, deep bark. Is it a huge guard dog? No. The big bark is coming from a small dog! Scottish terriers are little dogs that sound big.

Furry Fact
People call Scottish terriers Scotties for short.

SCOTTIES FROM SCOTLAND

The Scottish terriers come from Scotland. These dogs helped hunters. They chased small animals into dens and dug after them. Scotties still like to chase and dig.

Furry Fact
Some Scotties race in earthdog trials. They sniff for rats in tunnels.

DOUBLE COAT

Scottish terriers have a **double coat** of fur. The outer layer is stiff and wiry. Underneath is a soft coat. Their coats can grow down to the floor. They need haircuts.

Furry Fact

Scottie colors include black, wheaten, and brindle. Wheaten is a very light brown. Brindle means having streaks of other colors.

SCOTTIE SENSES

Scottie dogs have keen senses. Pointed ears hear quiet sounds. Their eyes see well. A long nose gives them a strong sense of smell. They have sharp teeth to grab small animals.

LEGS AND FEET

Short legs keep Scottish terriers close to the ground. Long belly fur can hide their feet. Running Scotties can look like they are rolling on wheels.

Furry Fact
Scotties are not good swimmers. Their legs are too short.

TRAINING

Scotties may be small, but they are **independent**. They must be trained to listen. Scotties are smart. These dogs like praise and rewards for doing a good job.

WATCHDOG

Scottish terriers are **alert**. They can make good watchdogs. These dogs bark to tell when a stranger is near. They sometimes howl.

PUPPIES

Scottie puppies look like little balls of fur. About five are born in a **litter**. Newborn pups have floppy ears. Their ears point up after about eight weeks.

LOYAL PETS

Scottish terriers are **loyal**. They like to be with their families. Even though they are small, Scotties want to keep their families safe. These dogs make great pets.

HOW DO YOU KNOW IT'S A SCOTTISH TERRIER?

pointed ears

long head

straight tail

double coat

short legs

WORDS TO KNOW

alert – being watchful and ready to act quickly

brindle – streaked with several colors

double coat – a coat of fur with two layers of different kinds of hair

independent – needing to do things on their own and in their own way

litter – a group of puppies born at the same time

loyal – to have a strong love for someone

wheaten – a very light brown color

LEARN MORE

Books

Gagne, Tammy. *West Highlands, Scotties, and Other Terriers*. Dog Encyclopedias. North Mankato, Minn.: Capstone Press, 2017.

Gray, Susan H. *Scottish Terriers*. All About Dogs. New York: AV2 by Weigl, 2017.

Websites

American Kennel Club: Scottish Terriers
http://www.akc.org/dog-breeds/scottish-terrier/

Friends of the Dog: Scottish Terrier
http://www.friendsofthedog.co.za/scottish-terrier.html

Scottish Terrier Club of America
http://www.stca.biz

INDEX